Zafu's Quest

A Child's Introduction to Meditation

By Fatima Ruiz

For my daughter
whose smile lights up my heart...

A special thank you to my family
for your support, encouragement & love

Zafu's Quest

A Child's Introduction to Meditation

By Fatima Ruiz

Editor : Esther Hershenhorn

Illustrator : Abira Das

© 2014
ISBN# 978-0-9909428-0-1
All rights reserved

The mysterious jungle of faraway Al-Kimia is home to the very special Mandala monkeys.

Especially special are the young Mandala from the east, west, and south, for on their Ninth Birthday they are sent on a Monkey Quest in search of the Golden Flower.

Legend has it that like magic, one whiff of three gathered petals can forever transform a monkey into any animal he or she likes.

Or, he can choose to remain a monkey and return home.

Legend also has it that only Prana the Tiger can guide you to this magical bloom.

But to release it's magic,
the young monkey must first learn the secret to meditation.

So it was that on the last night of his eighth year, Zafu tossed and turned. Elephants and tigers and even gazelles danced in his dreams.

It was on that first day of his ninth year, already far from home, Zafu met up with an elephant girl. "You're on your Monkey Quest, aren't you?" she asked. "I went on mine not long ago." Zafu's tail stilled.

"You were a monkey like me?" he asked.
"Yes, I'm Lali, from the Mandala in the east!"
Zafu's dark monkey eyes widened.

"If you were a Mandala monkey," he asked,
"why haven't you gone home?"
"Because I'm an elephant, silly! Once you transform
into a different jungle animal, you can't go home
because your family won't recognize you."

"Hmmmm..." thought Zafu. That fact surprised him.

"So, how do you like being an elephant, Lali?"

"It's the best! I go wherever I want, eat whatever I like, and play all day."

"I was thinking of becoming an elephant or possibly a tiger, maybe even a gazelle? I'm still not sure," Zafu shared.

"You're going to choose an elephant, I know it!" said Lali.
Lali really wanted a friend...

The two played for the rest of the day.
Once or twice, when Lali forgot she was an elephant and tried swinging from a tree branch, she fell flat on her bottom.
"Oops!" she said. "I'm not a monkey anymore!"
The two friends laughed.

Still, "Hmmm…" Zafu wondered.
Swinging was something
Zafu loved to do.

Lali couldn't wait to bring Zafu to her favorite place, Solutio Lake.

"I don't know how to swim! I'm scared, Lali!" Zafu shouted.

"You'll love the water!" Lali assured him. "Just still your body and allow it to float on the water."
Zafu closed his eyes and floated, all the while thinking about his monkey ways.

Zafu awoke tired and hungry but ready to continue his Quest. As he and Lali walked, they ran into a nervous gazelle.

"Monkey Quest! Monkey Quest! You're on your Monkey Quest! I know it! I'm Aneela from the west! I finished my Quest last summer, but now I want to go home! I miss my family!"

Zafu and Lali were very surprised.
Another Madala monkey!
Aneela quickly paused, then slowly took several
long deep breaths.
"What were you doing?" asked Zafu.
"Breathing helps my mind to stop racing,"
Aneela explained.
Zafu and Lali felt the air around them calm...

"We're searching for the Golden Flower," Lali shared.
"Do you remember where it is, Aneela?"
"No," answered Aneela, "only Prana can take you there.
I'm looking for him myself. I'm hoping he can
transform me back into a monkey! May I join you?"

"Sure!" Zafu blurted out. "I've always wondered what it would be like to be a gazelle." How eager Aneela was to show Zafu her gazelle ways, prancing about and teaching Zafu how to prance about too.

Except, prancing wasn't to Zafu's liking. Now he was absolutely certain he didn't want to be a gazelle either!

A tiger! That's what Zafu wanted to be! Tigers were brave and strong like him, he thought. Zafu scratched his monkey ears. He needed to be speak honestly.

"I think I'd like to be become a tiger," he announced. "Not an elephant or a gazelle."

Aneela became sad.
And Lali became mad!

"I can't believe my elephant ears! You want to transform into a tiger, Zafu? Tigers are big and mean and nobody likes them! If I saw a tiger right now, I would tell him just that. Elephants are wiser and much more likeable!" Lali hoofed the dirt and trumpeted loudly. "See!" she said. "I can be just as scary as any tiger!"

Zafu's legs and monkey tail froze.
His monkey eyes grew large.
"Oh, Zafu," Lali said,
"I was only pretending..."

Except... right then a
FEROCIOUS tiger jumped in front of them!
Lali and Aneela fainted on the jungle floor.
The tiger growled at Zafu.

"You're on your Monkey Quest!
I know this!"

Poor Zafu!
Tiger dragged him by the
scruff of his neck, deep,
then deeper into the
jungle, finally to a cave
beneath a waterfall.

"Are you-you-you go-go-go-ing to eat-eat me?" Zafu asked. He was so afraid of Tiger, he knew right then and there he did not want to transform into a scary tiger and frighten his friends.

It was then that the tiger revealed his true self. "I am Prana," he told Zafu. "Prana, the Tiger Guide. Now look about you. Behold, the Golden Flower!"

Zafu stood tall, finally in the presence of the most beautiful flower he'd ever seen. Its petals shimmered. Golden light poured from its center. And, oh, the scent! That sweet, sweet scent!

"Now sit, Zafu, and meditate through the night. Only then will you know which jungle animal you shall choose."

Again, poor Zafu! He knew not what to do.

"How does a monkey meditate?" he asked.
Prana looked Zafu in the eye.
"First," he said, "still your body. Then quiet your mind.
Finally open your heart. Only then can you allow the
golden light to flow inside of you."

Prana tore three petals
from the Golden Flower.
"Sniff once from these three
petals and you will become
the animal you choose to be."

Zafu did as he was told.
First he stilled his body as Lali had taught him at
Solutio Lake. Soon thoughts of his loving family,
his father, and his mother poured in.

Next he breathed deeply and slowly, quieting his
mind as Aneela had done. All he could think about
was how he missed his monkey ways, his monkey
friends and, most of all, his monkey family.

Finally, he opened his heart
as Prana had taught him.

"I love being a monkey!" he declared.
"I love being Zafu!" Zafu wondered no more.

"Are you ready to go home?" Tiana asked.
Zafu grinned. "Yes!" he answered.
"Take these petals to your family. While they no longer hold magical powers, they are your proof you found the Golden Flower."

Zafu wasted not a minute. He ran ran on his monkey legs and was almost home when, suddenly, Lali and Aneela appeared before him.

"You're going home, aren't you?" cried Lali.
Zafu nodded yes.

"Do you want to go home, too?" he asked.
Lali lowered her head.

"Yes," she sighed. "I love being an elephant,
but I miss my monkey family."

"Hmmmm..." Zafu thought while looking at the
three petals.

And so it was on the second day of Zafu's
Monkey Quest, Zafu made a second choice.

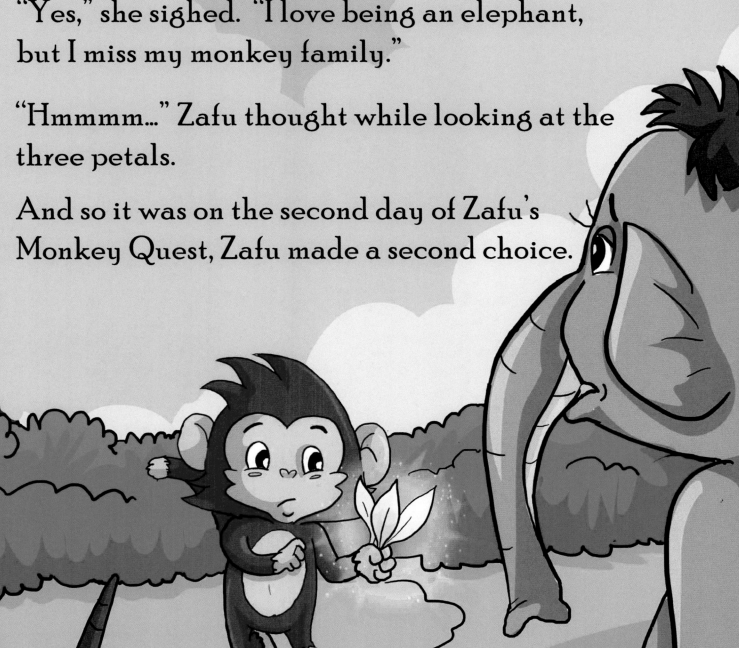

"Here," Zafu said, offering Lali one of his three petals and Aneela another. "Once your families see the petal, they'll know their daughters found the Golden Flower. They'll know their Lali even though she is an elephant. They'll know their Aneela even though she is a beautiful gazelle."

And legend has it
that's exactly what happened.

Meditation Instructions

When Zafu meditated with Prana, he stilled his body, quieted his mind and opened his heart to learn what he was seeking.

Would you like to meditate like Zafu?

Here's how:

Step 1-Close your eyes and keep your body as still as you possibly can.

Step 2 ~Breathe in deeply through your nose and hold your breath for 3 seconds, then slowly release your breath using only your nose. (Repeat 3-6 times)

Step 3-Finally, breathe in deeply through your nose but this time release your breath through your mouth, saying ha, ha, haaa.

Step 4-Now, keeping your eyes closed, imagine a fluffy white cloud surrounding your body.

Enjoy the peace you have created.